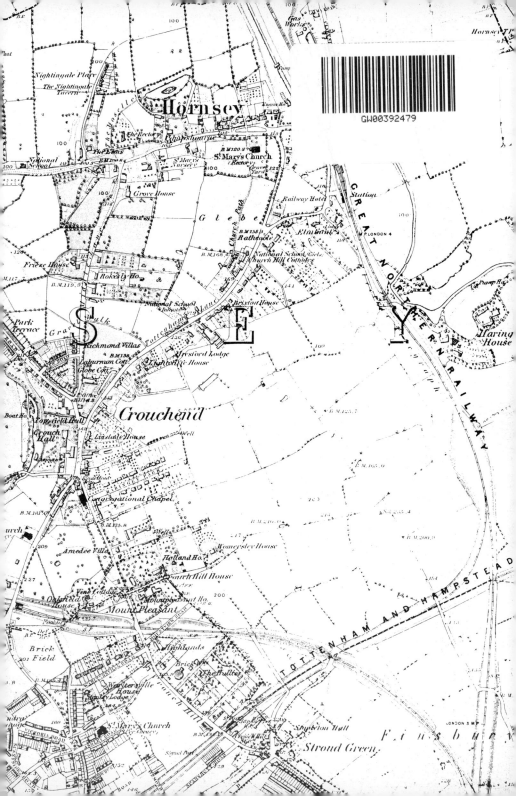

Maps Reproduced:

Inside front cover: 1873 Ordnance Survey
Inside back cover: 1920 Ordnance Survey

FOREST TO SUBURB
The Story of Hornsey Retold

By
Ken Gay

Published by Hornsey Historical Society

Hornsey Historical Society,
136 Tottenham Lane,
London N8 7EL

First published 1988
Second edition 1996
(with minor amendments)

Cover design: Robert Robertson
Production: Peter Curtis

Set in 10 point Times Roman
by Pennant Press

Printed and bound in Great Britain by
J.G. Bryson (Printer) Ltd.,
Huntingdon Works
156-164 High Road
East Finchley, London N2 9AS

ISBN 0 905794 04 4

Contents

COVER ILLUSTRATION:
The Unveiling on 22nd June, 1895 of Crouch End Clock Tower, built in his lifetime to honour H.R. Williams, chairman of Hornsey's Local Board for his successful campaign to preserve Highgate Woods. By courtesy of Bruce Castle Museum.

Preface

Hornsey has been absorbed into the northern suburbs of London and forms part of the London Borough of Haringey. Most of its inhabitants would regard themselves as Londoners. For much of its history though, Hornsey was a rural Middlesex parish, some 3,000 acres in extent, with its main settlements at Hornsey village, Crouch End, Muswell Hill and Highgate. Only in the latter half of the 19th century did urbanisation take place.

This short introductory essay aims to describe how Hornsey has been shaped and formed over the centuries. It has been written on behalf of the Hornsey Historical Society, membership of which is recommended to anyone interested in the area. It would not have been produced without the support of the society. In particular its writing and publication has been aided by those members of the society's publications committee who have commented on its contents, illustration and production, including Alan Aris, Peter Curtis, Susan Hector, Ian Murray, Joan Schwitzer and Malcolm Stokes.

Ken Gay
July 1988

Before the Norman Conquest

Hornsey is a name of Anglo-Saxon origin and we know nothing about it as a place until medieval times. But geographical factors and historical events before the Saxon invasions have helped to shape Hornsey's history.

When the Romans invaded Britain in 43 AD they established Londinium as a trading post on the Thames, taking advantage of natural features. Two gravel hills on the north side of the marshy river estuary where the tidal waters turned allowed settlement, and a similar gravel hill on the south side of the river provided a crossing point for a road system. Londinium became a great port because of the natural advantages of the site, which offered a deep river ideally situated for trade with Europe, the Baltic, and the Mediterranean. This nodal point attracted markets, wealth, people, power and government. London was to become a very great city.

As we all know, the territory around London has become dominated subsequently by the city's needs. Settlements close to it were to be lived in or used by Londoners and ultimately they were to become part of London's built environment. Hornsey's history as a place some five miles north is inevitably part of this story.

Other geographical factors meant that Hornsey's early population was never to be very large. A significant feature when the Romans came, mentioned by their historian Tacitus, is the great forest north of the Thames. The terrain here is dominated by the cold clay of the Thames basin, which was favourable to the growth of trees in prehistoric times, so that forests of lime, oak, elm, alder, pine, birch and other species developed. Coldfall and Highgate woods are remnants of this great forest. Although from earliest times, long before the Romans arrived, people began to clear the forest, its vastness was to impede agricultural development. Clearance of trees in Hornsey was to go on well into the 17th and 18th centuries.

The clay soil favourable to tree growth was not so good for arable farming and this explains the small population. Settlers cleared trees and started subsistence farming but for most of its history Hornsey has been sparsely populated. Eventually its main land use was pasture and grass, to meet London's needs.

The hilly nature of the terrain helped make Hornsey a rural place seen later as one of its charms, with its landscape of trees, hedges and fine hill views. Main traffic routes tended to skirt the area, with the Ermine Street route following the Lee valley on the east, on the line of Tottenham High Road, and Watling Street to Chester via Kilburn on the west. East-west roads connecting these two Roman roads would have passed through Hornsey — though they have not been identified — and in medieval times a road to the north developed through Crouch End and Muswell Hill and another one through Highgate.

No evidence of Roman settlement has been discovered closer than Edmonton and Enfield, though that is not to say that it did not occur. In Highgate Woods the remains of a small Roman pottery site, probably operating on a seasonal basis have been excavated. A quarter of a mile away, in Cranley Gardens, a pot was unearthed in a garden in 1928 containing over 650 Roman coins and a silver spoon. Other Roman coins have been found in scattered places in Hornsey.

Serving in the Roman legions were Teutonic peoples from northern Europe. After the 5th century collapse of the Roman empire people from northern Europe increasingly migrated to these islands, crossing by boat and possibly using the rivers to make their way inland. They invaded, settled and farmed. Place names in Essex, Middlesex and Hertfordshire are nearly all Anglo Saxon in origin and this includes Hornsey. It is derived from the Old English words *Heringes-hege*, meaning the enclosure of Haering or Hering's people. Hornsey, Harringay and other spellings of the name derive from this root. One of these forms was chosen in 1965 to name the new London Borough of Haringey. Dr. Madge, the local historian who researched the name's origin, lists some 150 ways the name has been spelt in documents from the 12th century onwards.

Anglo Saxon immigrants gave their name to Hornsey, although it is not known whether a Romano-British settlement might not have existed there before that. Because of the absence of records little is known of the early medieval period but it can be assumed that landed estates and early forms of local government were established including an hierarchical system of tenure which was to be taken over and named as 'manorial' by the Normans after 1066 AD.

The Anglo Saxon immigrants were pagans, but were to be Christianised after the arrival in 597 AD of a mission from the Pope headed by St. Augustine. The Bishopric of London was re-established in 604 AD (after an earlier Roman Christian period) with Mellitus, companion of St. Augustine, as first Bishop of London. The cathedral of St. Paul was established on a hill in the city. Both Bishop of London and the Dean and Chapter of St. Paul's became local landowners, with the Bishop of London becoming lord of the manor of Hornsey.

Over the centuries much land was given to or acquired by the church and it was to hold most of the land in Middlesex, with no large aristocratic landowner near the capital posing a threat to the monarch. The county of Middlesex emerges as the smallest of the ancient pre-Norman shires. Its name denotes the Middle Saxons, possibly an offshoot of the East Saxons who gave their name to Essex.

The church tower still standing in Hornsey High Street denotes the location of the medieval parish church, first recorded in the 13th century. How long before that a church existed on the site is not known. A Christian church might well have been located here in Saxon times, even possibly on an existing pagan religious site, possibly on the hill behind the church, but this is pure conjecture. It could be that the original enclosure, denoted by the name Hornsey, was made here in the forest, where Hornsey village was to be established.

At some time unknown, Hornsey parish boundaries were established, as well as those of Hornsey manor. The boundaries are assumed to have been unchanged until the end of the 19th century. Most of the parish was in the manor or Hornsey, but the southern portion was occupied by Brownswood manor, with the Prebendary of Brownswood of St. Paul's chapter as the lord. Later Hornsey manor was to see Topsfield and Farnefields manors formed by sub-infeudation.

Among parishes adjacent to Hornsey was Tottenham to the east and north. In the late 19th century this was to be divided into Wood Green and Tottenham urban districts which later became borough councils. In the 20th century these two boroughs joined with the borough of Hornsey to form the London Borough of Haringey.

Finchley, to the west of Hornsey, was about the same size parish, and also had the Bishop of London as its manorial lord. His hunting park was to stretch across both parishes. To the south west of Hornsey were the parishes of St. Pancras and Islington and to the south the parish of Stoke Newington which had embedded in it detached portions of the parish of Hornsey.

Medieval Hornsey

The first recorded references to settlements are in 1152 (Muswell Hill), 1227 (Highgate), 1291 (Hornsey church) and 1407 (Stroud Green). A medieval road system developed along with settlement, perhaps enlarging tracks established by earlier peoples. These roads were unpaved and ill defined and often impassable, because of deterioration under adverse weather conditions, the impact of hooves and wheels and the lack of any administration for upkeep.

Hornsey church is first referred to in 1291 when assessed for Papal taxation. The first known reference to the rector, who has always been appointed by the Bishop of London, is in 1303. A Bishop of London's will of that date bequeathed silver plate to Walter de London, Rector of the Church 'at Haringeye'. The tower which remains to-day can be dated by the Bishops of London's arms on it to 1500 but the structure is likely to be earlier.

Hornsey Church depicted in 1791 some 40 years before the medieval nave and south aisle were demolished. The tower was subsequently heightened. Too small for Hornsey's growing population and in disrepair the old church and graveyard were affected by water seepage from the nearby New River. By courtesy of Highgate Literary and Scientific Institution.

The rest of the medieval parish church of St. Mary was demolished in 1832 when a Gothic-styled Suffolk-white brick church designed by George Smith replaced it. In 1889 a new, non-oriented perpendicular-style church designed by James Brooks was built outside the graveyard on the present site of St. Mary's Infant School, whilst the other church remained unused. The nave of the 1832 church was demolished in 1927 whilst the 1889 church survived until 1969. The parish still exists as part of a linked modern parish known as St. Mary with St. George, based on St. George's church created in Edwardian times and located since 1959 in a new church building on the corner of Park Road and Cranley Gardens. Details of the history of St. Mary's as a church building are given by Ian Murray in *The Old Parish Church of Hornsey* and in other booklets published by The Friends of Hornsey Church Tower.

8

No manor house for Hornsey is recorded and possibly with an absentee episcopal lord of the manor none ever existed. Earliest meetings of manorial courts were probably held at Stepney, in the bishop's barony, but later at Highgate. Court records survive for 1318-19, 1376 and for many later years, with gaps, down to modern times. The text of them for the years 1603-1701 were published in printed form by the Marcham brothers and show the range of civil matters covered. Conveyance of land and communal rights in particular came under their control.

Crouch End derives its name from words meaning 'cross end'. Possibly a cross was erected here for ecclesiastical or parish business. Or its name might indicate that this is where roads meet. A road from London entered the parish, passing through **Stroud Green**, a name indicating marshy scrub land (where no settlement is known of, except for Stapleton Hall and Japan House, until the 19th century), went over the Hogs Back ridge, passed through Crouch End and continued up Muswell Hill and along the line of present day Colney Hatch Lane. Another road from the south also went through Crouch End and continued along Tottenham Lane towards Tottenham. Crouch End's name might derive from the crossing of these two routes.

Local people know that the foot of Muswell Hill is prone to flooding, due to stream water off the Highgate Woods ridge and it might be that this was one factor which caused the Tudor historian Norden to record that the road to the north via Crouch End became impassable in bad weather. An alternative route developed from Holloway up Highgate Hill in the west, with the Bishop of London allowing travellers to cross his hunting park at the top of Highgate Hill.

Highgate developed in consequence as a settlement on the boundary of Hornsey parish, its name deriving from the gate in the boundary hedge to the park. At the gate a chapel was established, granted by the Bishop of London in 1387 to William Lichfield, a hermit. Repair of the roads was by the hermits. A toll was extracted by the Bishop of London from those using the new road, as first recorded in 1318. He farmed it out by 1390, indicating that use of the road was increasing. In time a gatehouse was built, arched across the road, the meeting place of a manorial court. The site is now occupied by the Gatehouse public house and Highgate school chapel. Within a few centuries Highgate was to develop along its highways, with a number of aristocratic residents, a wayside chapel, a grammar school, and was to be the largest and wealthiest settlement in Hornsey, albeit only partly in the parish.

Muswell Hill becomes identifiable in 1152 when the Bishop of London granted over 64 acres of land here for use as a dairy farm to the Augustinian Nuns of the Priory of St. Mary at Clerkenwell. The land between the road to the north (now

9

Colney Hatch Lane) and the parish boundary with Tottenham to the east of it was probably manorial waste. This is an early example of the Hornsey area serving the needs of London.

According to Norden a Scottish king was cured of an illness by drinking the water from a spring on this land. This is not so surprising as might first appear, since the neighbouring manor of Tottenham was held at this time by Scottish royalty; Malcolm IV is identified as the likely king. The nuns built a chapel by the water, and the well with its curative powers became the subject of pilgrimage during the Middle Ages. Colney Hatch Lane, along which the pilgrims passed, was earlier known as Halliwick Lane, which might be a place name reference to holy well, although Halliwick is also the name of the manor to the north in Friern Barnet.

The well gave its name to the place, for Muswell derives as a name from the Old English words meaning 'mossy spring'. The place name Pinnes Knoll, in variant spellings, which might have meant the hill of someone called Pinn by which the area was referred to was displaced. Muswell Hill was established as the local name by the end of the 15th century, although Pinnes Knoll is still also being mentioned as a name in the manor court rolls for the 17th century, but not so marked on maps.

Two thirds of the parish probably remained wooded in medieval times. Economic life revolved around the manorial system with oxen and later horses used for subsistence agriculture which would have been carried out by the very small numbers of local people. Increasingly, the manors were used for pasture, with dairying and stock raising and grass crops. The woods were exploited for pig raising, and for timber by coppicing, whereby deciduous trees are cut down to ground level and then allowed to regrow. The only local industry seems to have been making bricks and tiles. Trades related to stock raising such as butchers and tanners plus blacksmiths, wheelwrights, harness makers and saddlers were to be needed as society developed.

The hunting park developed by the Bishop of London in his Hornsey and Finchley manorial lands would have been by royal licence. The first known reference is in 1227. The park was banked, ditched and hedged to preserve the beasts of the chase. In 1241 and 1242 there are references to deer in the park, gifts of the king. Surviving portions of the park hedge in Lyttleton Playing Fields have been dated to the mid 13th century. Some 380 acres of the 1,070 acres of woods were in Finchley and the rest in Hornsey. Malcolm Stokes in *HHS Bulletin no. 25* traces the likely boundaries and describes the history of the park. His article mentions that the bishop had a lodge in the park, sited in the centre of what to-day is Highgate golf course, and situated where the boundary between

Finchley and Hornsey runs. The lodge was visited by Edward I in 1305 and was recorded as being in ruins in 1441. In due course hunting declined, though the Bishop retained hunting rights until 1662.

The growing traffic on the road through Highgate included livestock being brought to the markets of London. The most recent estimates put the city's population in 1300 at about 100,000, higher by far than previously thought and making it larger than other medieval cities such as Cologne, Ghent, Bruges and Rome, and probably second only to Paris. Only the Black Death was to reduce it. In 1300 London probably had between 5,000 and 10,000 shops and in Cheapside alone there were 4,000 stallholders in at least 80 covered bazaars.

As London grew its disadvantages to merchants who lived and worked from their own houses and mansions became more obvious. The city was crowded, noisy and insanitary, and did not offer the fresh water, the quietness and the clean air to be found in the surrounding countryside. Thus developed the essential break between place of work and place of residence that Londoners now take for granted. Londoners began to buy properties outside the city, either as alternative places of residence or as investment opportunities. Land would also be acquired for commercial purposes such as for grazing stock to be fattened up for the London market.

As we are reminded by John Fisher in *The A to Z of Elizabethan London* (London Topographical Society 1979) which reproduces the Agas map showing London in the 1560s, it was a relatively small and compact city, packed into an area barely exceeding one square mile. 'By to-day's standards there was little suburban sprawl and London wall — still intact at this period — acted as a sharp dividing line between town and country on the northern and eastern sides of the City'. It was the outward movement of Londoners which was to be the story of succeeding centuries.

Developments from the 15th to the 19th century

The essential pre-condition for a residence outside the city was some form of transport. The better-off would use their own coach and horses to take them to their country estates. These heavy vehicles with iron clad wheels needed four to six horses to make their way over the rutted roads. Similar vehicles began to be used for an increasing number of coach services. De Laune's *Present State of London* (1681) records that 119 coach services were then operating, fifty within a 25 mile radius of London, although speeds were only about four miles per hour. Poorer people travelled by carrier's wagon, a long, canvas-topped vehicle, pulled by as many as eight horses.

The wealthy carved out sizeable estates. Amongst these was Mattysons, marked on the 1619 map of Tottenham parish made for the then lord of the manor, the Earl of Dorset, but situated at Muswell Hill near Colney Hatch Lane. Mattysons was the seat of Sir Julius Caesar (d. 1636) Master of the Rolls and Chancellor of the Exchequer to James I and descendant of an Italian doctor who had attended Queen Elizabeth I. It was in this nobleman's arms that Francis Bacon, Viscount St. Albans, was to die in 1626 at the Earl of Arundel's house at Highgate. Caesar's wife was a niece of Francis Bacon. The death of Bacon (1561-1626), an extraordinary man to whom the works of Shakespeare have been attributed, was said to be due to a chill caught by stuffing a fowl with snow in an attempt to study the effect of cold in delaying putrefaction, aggravated by damp sheets on the bed to which he was taken.

Highgate, with its fine situation, attracted aristocratic and wealthy residents. In 1664 it already contained 161 houses whilst the rest of Hornsey contained only 62. Courtiers acquiring houses included Lord Howard, Sir William Hatton and Sir Thomas Cornwallis, whose son probably built Arundel House, visited by Elizabeth I and James I. Other larger houses included Lauderdale House, where Nell Gwynn is reputed to have stayed, Bisham House and Dorchester House, all in the parish of St. Pancras. Surviving still is Cromwell House, built on the Hornsey side of Highgate Hill c 1638 by Sir Richard Sprignell (d. 1659). Another nearby resident was Sir John Wollaston (d. 1658) who acquired the lordship of the manor of Hornsey in 1647 in the Interregnum — when the country had no monarch. Another Lord Mayor was Sir William Rowe (d. 1593) who had a house at Muswell Hill.

In the wake of the Reformation of the English church (dissolution of religious houses 1536-39, first English prayer book 1549, Act of Uniformity 1559, services in English 1569) there had been changes in religious attitudes. The Civil War period of the 1640s and 1650s exacerbated change and saw the growth of congregationalism, presbyterianism, the Quakers and other sects, particularly amongst traders and other middle class people. These groups were out of favour after the Restoration in 1660.

Highgate, the home of many parliamentarians, was just beyond the limits imposed by the 1665 Five Mile Act which had the effect of preventing nonconformist chapels being built within five miles of a town. This restrictive act was part of the Clarendon Code of laws which accompanied the restoration of the monarchy. Highgate became a natural resort for dissenters, with John Storey licensed as a presbyterian at his home in 1672. George Fox (1624-91) was entertained at Highgate by William Mead in 1677 and 1678 and a Meeting House was said to have been founded in Southwood Lane in 1662. In the 18th century old and new meeting houses stood each side of the Lane, one described as

Southwood Lane photographed circa 1921. On the right is Highgate Tabernacle and on the left the Wollaston-Pauncefoot almhouses.

Presbyterian and the other as Methodist.

The Presbyterian meeting house was sold to the Baptists in 1814 and later rebuilt as a 'tabernacle'; it was acquired in 1977 by Highgate School to extend accommodation for pupils. The other meeting house became Highgate Congregational Church before the present building, now the United Reformed Church, was built in Pond Square.

The exact origin and date of many houses and estates in the parish is not known, although some survived into the 19th century and even beyond. Stapleton Hall, for example, has survived in altered form in Stapleton Hall Road, Stroud Green; in 1988 it was rebuilt as residential flats.
First recorded in 1557 and extended and rebuilt in 1609, it has date stone and panelling with the initials of Sir Thomas Stapleton who was among 90 or more Londoners who held copyhold land in Hornsey in the 17th century. Harringay

House, possibly also of Tudor origin, rebuilt in 1792 by Edward Gray, linen draper of London, stood on the east side of the parish near Green Lanes until the 1880s when its lands were used for terraced housing and it was demolished.

The Grove, on the north side of Muswell Hill, was also probably Tudor in origin, although a new house was erected in the late 18th century. For some ten years it was tenanted by Topham Beauclerk, a descendant of Charles II by Nell Gwynn. Among his friends this aristocrat numbered Dr. Samuel Johnson (1709-84) who was one of the visitors to the Grove. Beauclerk married Lady Di, divorced wife of Lord Bolingbroke. Her portrait by Reynolds is to be seen at Kenwood, Highgate. Beauclerk, a rake and a gambler was also a scholar, with a fine house in Bloomsbury containing a large library. At the Grove he built a laboratory for chemical experiments and an observatory. The fame of the house was such that tickets were issued to gain admission. The house was demolished in the 1870s but the estate grounds, added to Alexandra Park, still keep the name.

Development out of London tended to be along the line of the main roads. By the 1720s Daniel Defoe is writing in his *Tour through England and Wales:*

'Newington, Tottenham, Edmonton and Enfield stand all in a line N. from the city; the encrease of buildings is so great in them all that they seem to a traveller to be one continu'd street; especially Tottenham and Edmonton, and in them all, the new buildings so far exceed the old, especially in the value of them, and the figure of the inhabitants, that the fashion of the towns is quite altered'.

Describing Tottenham, Defoe writes: 'Here is at this town a small but pleasant seat of the Earl of Colerain; his lordship...has a very good estate here, extending from this town to Muzzle-hill and almost to High-gate'. The Earl of Coleraine was lord of Tottenham manor and the estate consisted of the manor lands, including Bruce Castle, the manor house. In 1789, for financial reasons, these lands were auctioned. Still surviving in Tottenham High Road to-day are some fine Georgian houses which remain from the time when it was a smart place for an out-of-town residence.

Describing Highgate, Defoe says: 'there is a very beautiful house built by the late Sir William Ashurst, on the very summit of the hill, and with a view from the very lowest windows over the whole vale, to the city; And that so eminently, that they see the very ships passing up and down the river for 12 or 15 miles below London. The Jews have particularly fixt upon this town for their country retreats, and some of them are very wealthy; they live here in good figure, and have several trades particularly depending upon them, especially butchers of their own to supply them with provisions kill'd their own way; also, I am told, they have a private synagogue here'.

Not only did the rich have houses at Highgate, but as the road became increasingly used by drovers and travellers large inns were established. Houses began to line North Road, Southwood Lane and Hornsey Lane. Soon after 1664 a forge was in existence at the corner of the high road and Pond Square, facing Angel Row — and was to survive until 1896. In 1767 the road through Highgate was widened and the narrow arched gatehouse with its two storeys across the main road was demolished. On the chapel field in Southwood Lane, Wollaston's almshouses were built; both chapel and almshouses were to be enlarged in the 18th century. The traffic stimulated public house trade and the inn keepers objected when, to avoid the steepness of Highgate Hill, a by-pass road was proposed.

Nevertheless the by-pass — a feature which the New Road on the northern outskirts of London had pioneered in 1757 — was built in 1813. It was named Archway Road after the earlier arched tunnel, which collapsed and was replaced by the present cutting through Highgate Hill, with the Archway bridge to carry Hornsey Lane across it. It was probably the first flyover in Britain. Its construction is described by Arnold Lynch in *HHS Bulletin no. 23.*

By this time the turnpike system of tolls was being used to provide an upgraded road system in a land where the pace of economic change was quickening. For not only did the 17th and 18th centuries see a spread of estates into Hornsey, it also saw the landscape change.

Between Tudor times and the beginning of the 19th century the area of Hornsey farmlands slowly increased as the woods and wastes were developed. Over this period the woodlands were halved. In 1540 the proportion of land farmed was little more than a quarter of the district. But by 1820 over two thirds were used. Farming did not mean arable farming; as Lysons said in 1794, little of the lands here were under the plough. Dairy farming and hay were important, with hay increasingly supplied to feed the growing number of horses used in London for transport and other work. Migrant workers were engaged in haymaking. Booth, of the gin manufacturing family and Crouch End resident, kept sheep on his Shepherds Hill estate and Thomas Rhodes of Tottenham Wood farm was aiming to increase his herd to 1,000 cows in the early 19th century.

Changes in society included new ways of controlling local affairs. From Tudor times onwards local government moved away from manorial courts. The need to deal with the destitute led to the 1601 Poor Law which put responsibility for relief of the poor on the parish vestries, with a poor rate being levied. To avoid some places being overburdened, Laws of Settlement required that every person coming into a parish must have a certificate showing where he was born, apprenticed or legally settled — so that he could be sent back if he became a burden on the parish.

Parishes were also responsible for the maintenance of the church fabric and for the upkeep of the highways, for both of which it also charged rates. The vestry had the duty of appointing local people as officials to deal with these problems, including churchwardens, constables, surveyors of the highways and overseers of the poor. Under a statute labour system every parishioner had to give six days labour a year to help repair the roads, but many were reluctant to undertake this or to take up parish offices and paid a rate in lieu of service.

Crime was handled by local unpaid Justices of the Peace who also approved vestry expenditure and appointments. Professional judges travelled to county assizes to handle more serious criminal cases.

In Hornsey, manorial courts' activity went on longer than in many other places and were, in fact, to continue to modern times. But Hornsey vestry, first mentioned in 1688, had its officials and was responsible for the poor, highways and other matters as the surviving vestry minute books reveal. Kept in an iron chest in St. Mary's until the church's demolition in 1969 these records are now held in the Greater London Record Office. Richard Samways of the GLRO in an article in *HHS Bulletin no. 28* describes some of the vestry's activities in the 18th century.

Hornsey was unusual in having two sets of churchwardens, surveyors and overseers of the poor, one for 'Hornsey Side' and the other for 'Highgate Side' serving the two main communities of the parish. Meeting at first about three times a year, and then more frequently, usually under the chairmanship of the rector, the general conduct of business was in the hands of the vestry clerk. The minutes survive from the year 1739 when the vestry clerk was John Henry Bailey, paid an annual fee of four guineas. An apothecary of the poor occurs from 1750 and a workhouse master from 1743. Another official was the beadle. In 1774 he was appointed at a salary of five guineas and was given a new coat and hat every three years. As well as supervising the poor he kept order in the church and cleaned the building — from 1792 he was given an allowance for brooms.

In 1730 the parish leased a house in Hornsey Lane for a workhouse and in 1735 acquired one acre of land in Hornsey High Street where a new building stood by 1743. By 1827 this workhouse had been extended and held 83 inhabitants, while 104 were on outdoor relief. A vestry minute of 1782 says that the wearing apparel of the poor of the parish is to be of one colour and they are to wear a badge of HP upon their arms. Churchwardens and overseers would go once yearly to visit children put out as apprentices by the parish and be allowed £1.15.0d for their expenses.

In 1803 a cage or village lock-up was placed in the workhouse garden on the one acre site, and stocks by the church (The lock-up became the mortuary in 1868, replaced in 1886 by the coroners court — not far away from the site to-day). In Highgate a cage had been established by 1720 and in 1770 stood on the south west side of the High Street, its cost to be shared with St. Pancras parish. It was next to the watch-house opposite Southwood Lane where a fire station was also established in 1811.

In the second half of the 19th century the vestry was to give way to new forms of local government in the shape of local councils, presaged by boards set up to deal with specific problems such as highways and health. A new Poor Law in 1834 was one of the first changes brought about by legislation. From 1837 Hornsey's poor were dealt with by the Edmonton Poor Law Union, covering a wider area. Hornsey's local workhouse was demolished.

Under the 1835 General Highways Act a highways board was established in 1854 by the vestry. Reorganised in 1855, it then employed a salaried clerk, rate collector, assistant surveyor and public health inspector as well as highway surveyors and had reduced the highways rate to 6d in the £. The Act abolished the statutory duty of parishioners to repair the roads by their own labour and repealed statutory restrictions on wheels, weights and numbers of horses which could be used on roads — which had been attempts to make traffic suit the roads, rather than the roads to suit the traffic. At this time the art of roadmaking was greatly improved by John Macadam and Thomas Telford and the average speed of coaches rose from five to eight miles per hour, or higher. In 1836 there were 3,000 coaches running in the country, requiring 150,000 horses and giving employment to some 30,000 people.

The parliamentary enclosures and after

Improved roads were one aspect of the industrial revolution which Britain pioneered in the years 1760-1830, a period of acute change. From being predominantly agricultural, with a small population, mainly with a low standard of living by to-day's standards and without political power, the country was to alter into a manufacturing nation with a large population, great urban centres, vastly increased wealth for the middle classes, greater social mobility and ultimately political democracy.

The population increase, from about 6m in the early 18th century to 14m by 1831 and 32.5m by 1901 (it is about 55m to-day) was particularly to affect isolated areas such as Hornsey parish, which was to be altered by the growth of the great urban centre of London. The capital was to increase in size from about one million at the beginning of the 19th century to about four million by its end.

The general population increase in the country seemed to justify more intensive use of the land, employing new methods. One aspect of the change was the movement to enclose 'wastes' and common lands. In 1647 some 600 acres of Hornsey were commons. Common land lay between Muswell Hill and St. James's Lane, bordered Tetherdown and Fortis Green, and was extensive at Southwood Common, Highgate. There was also waste of the manors of Topsfield and Brownswood and at Stroud Green. The commons were used for pasturing livestock, especially by the poor who also took away gravel, loam, fern, furze and turf. The poor also tended to encroach on the commons by building places to live on them. 'Illegal' cottages were built at Southwood Common, Fortis Green and Muswell Hill.

From the 18th century onwards commons throughout the country were enclosed by separate local acts of parliament and divided amongst local landowners, a portion being given to the poor and clergy. Between 1760 and 1844 there were about 4,000 such Acts, affecting some 6m acres.

The Act for Hornsey was given royal assent in 1813, with the Award operative from 1816. The preamble to the Act reads:

'Whereas there are in the parish of Hornsey in the County of Middlesex divers commons and waste lands containing together by estimation four hundred acres or thereunto. And whereas the Right Reverend Father in God John Lord Bishop of London in right of his see is Lord of the Manor of Hornsey in the Parish of Hornsey aforesaid and as such is intitled to soil of the commons and waste lands within the said manor

And whereas the said Lord Bishop of London is Patron of the Rectory and Rector thereof and as such is entitled to certain tythes arising and payable from out of and in respect of the said commons and waste lands or to some modus, composition or other payment in lieu thereof and is also entitled to certain rights of common in over and upon the same in respect of such inclosed Glebe lands and rectorial homestead

And whereas the said John Lord Bishop of London in right of his said See is Patron of the Prebend of Brownswood formed in the Cathedral Church of St. Paul's in London and the Rev. George Secker, Clerk, is Prebendary and is in right thereof Lord of the Manor of Brownswood within the said Parish of Hornsey and as such is entitled to all the soil of all the commons and waste lands within the said manor of Brownswood and the same is demised by him to Elizabeth Willan etc....

And whereas the Right Honourable William, Earl of Mansfield, the said Lord Bishop of London, the said George Secker, Edward Gray, Esq., and others are the owners and proprietors of divers enclosed lands, tenements and hereditaments within the said Parish of Hornsey in respect thereof and they are entitled to Rights of Commons, of Pasture and other rights in over and upon the said commons and waste land...And whereas the said Commons and Waste Lands are in their present state incapable of any considerable improvement but the same if divided and enclosed might be greatly improved......May it therefore Please your Majesty That it may be Enacted......'

Under the Award the poor were allowed 12½ acres at Irish corner (where Hornsey parish abutted Friern Barnet parish by Colney Hatch Lane), one acre at Wood Lane, Highgate and two copyhold allotments of 3½ acres at Fortis Green. The bishop received 30 acres, the prebendary of Brownswood 24 acres, the rector of Hornsey 46½ acres, and the copyhold landowners the rest. To keep the beauty of Hornsey village some common used for grazing there was not enclosed, so preserving a wide village High Street which survives to-day.

Perhaps one unintended effect of the enclosures was to make more land available for building. Between the establishment of wealthy estates and the building of rows of terraced houses there is a stage of suburban development in the 19th century which should not be overlooked. This was the spread of villas and detached houses in smaller estates for the middle classes. Many of these villas survived only a short time and were replaced by terraced roads before the century was out.

The early 19th century villas still existing in Fortis Green, near the boundary with Finchley were built following the Enclosure Award. The broad common-lined road was reduced to its present narrow size. A similar Enclosure Act for Finchley was passed in 1811. Villas were also built along the western side of Colney Hatch Lane, a few of which still survive.

Pleasant villas were established on Crouch Hill, Crouch End Hill and Mount Pleasant on the ridge south of Crouch End. Amongst the earliest of these was Holland House, a three-storeyed bow fronted villa erected after 1781, illustrated in Hassell's *Rides and Walks.* Oakfield Villa and Oakfield House were among other new estates at Crouch End. Amongst the villas and farms was a small village centre. The bakery, and an associated post office receiving house existed and to-day Dunn's the bakers continues on the site in a building which carries the date 1850, a sculptured wheatsheaf and the initials WM which stood for William Muddiman, the founder. At the foot of Crouch Hill stood the smithy and the village pub, the Kings Head. Where the Town Hall forecourt now is was a farm building of the Crouch Hall estate which had been used as a chapel, first by the Baptists from 1806 and later by other denominations. The Anglicans rented it from 1844 till 1862, added a tower in 1851 and cupola and Gothic windows but left in 1863 when Christ Church was built. Later known as Broadway Hall it survived until 1925 as did adjacent weatherboarded Lake Villa. Here too was the village pump.

At Hornsey village the rectory was rebuilt and National schools established, for boys in Priory Road and for girls in Tottenham Lane. To the west,towards the foot of Muswell Hill, the Warner family rebuilt their house as The Priory, in Gothic style in the 1820s, some of the fittings coming from demolished Wanstead House in Essex. The house gave its name to Priory Road. On previous common land on the south east side of Muswell Hill a pub, now known as The Victoria Stakes, was built and three adjacent villas, and above them the Avenue House estate was established, also containing Rookfield House and a cottage to be renamed after a poem written by the Irish poet Thomas Moore, *Lalla Rookh,* published whilst he was in occupation.

The increasing number of villas at Muswell Hill, with cottagers making up the community, led to the district being given its own church of St. James's in 1842 on a site given by Henry Warner, which it still occupies, although the church is rebuilt. In 1850 the National School of St. James's was opened at the near end of Fortis Green to save children the journey to Hornsey. The new church was but one of seven which were to be formed out of the old parish of St. Mary's in the next decades. Already in 1832 Highgate had acquired St. Michael's for a growing congregation for which the old chapel-of-ease, which had relieved local residents of a journey to the parish church in Hornsey or at St. Pancras, was inadequate.

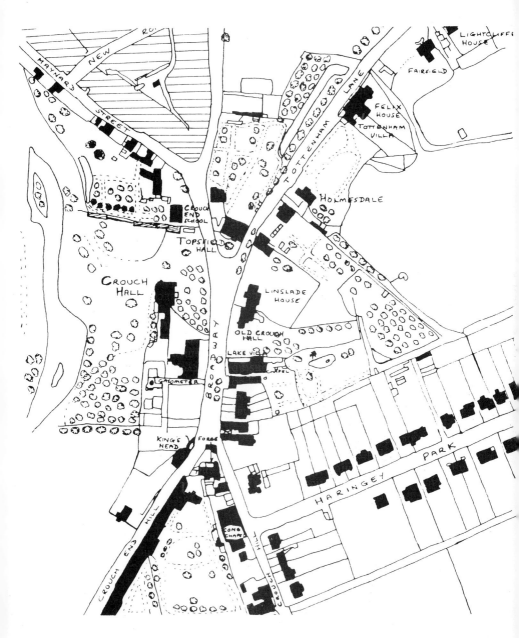

Crouch End Village *Based on a sketch map by W. Marcham. By courtesy of*
M.J. Morrison.

21

Christ Church at Crouch End was built in 1863 on land donated by Charles Scrase Dickens.

Muswell Hill, with its natural advantages, would at this time have been a fine place for a middle class family to live. A glimpse of this is given in the nostalgic reminiscences of Frederic Harrison (1831-1923), author and philosopher in his *Autobiographic Memoirs:*

'My earliest recollections for the first years of my life are entirely those of the country, and of a very beautiful country — green, shady and smokeless, although within reach of the city and now quite engulphed (sic) in the advancing suburbs of London. We lived in a pretty cottage, on the crest of Muswell Hill, just opposite the big pond which stood in the square at the three cross ways. The spot in the eighteen thirties was a beautiful and peaceful village, knowing none but rustic sights and sounds, and keeping the ways and notions of the countryside. My memory as a child is fragrant with the quiet sleepy strolls of babies and nurses, innocent happily of perambulators and modern toys, through flowery meadows and shady copses. How well I can remember the limpid stillness of the Muswell and the knolls where the cowslip and the violet grew under the oaks on the region now covered by the Alexandra Palace and its grounds. We would wander all day there and meet no one but a carter or a milkmaid. Hornsey Village and Highgate were the utmost limit of our excursions and our principal experience of town life....'

Highgate, mentioned by Harrison as a town, had become more sedate after the opening of Archway Road in 1813 and the loss of through traffic in the village centre. Holly Lodge, later famous as the country home of Angela Burdett Coutts, was built in 1809 on West Hill. The Grove was extended from 1832 and road realignment, south of a unified and tidied-up pond, in 1845 formed South Grove. In 1839 Highgate Literary and Scientific Institution was founded and developed as an axis for Highgate's social and cultural life. From 1830 the free Grammar school, founded by Sir Roger Cholmley began to introduce fees and to move towards being a fee-paying public school. It put up new school buildings and later acquired land for playing fields. St. Michael's National school was first built in Southwood Lane in 1833 to cater for poor local boys and to absorb the girl's charity school started in the 18th century in the centre of the Wollaston-Pauncefort almshouses alongside, and in 1852 moved into a new school in North Road designed by architect Anthony Salvin, who had also designed St. James's National School.

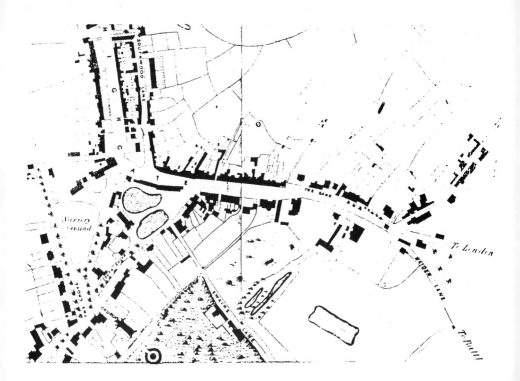

Highgate Village *From Frederick Prickett's History of Antiquities of Highgate, Middlesex 1842.*

The Archway road had stimulated development near it, with two new public houses (The Wellington of c. 1812 and The Woodman of 1828) and more houses were built along North Hill, Southwood Lane and Hornsey Lane. But the expansion of Highgate to the north was hampered by Lord Mansfield's Manor Farm and on its west by his Kenwood estate. As the 19th century progressed Highgate was to be developed mainly on its south-east side under pressures which were to lead to a total change for the old Hornsey parish.

23

Victorian expansion

In the first half of the 19th century Hornsey was a place where Londoners could take a day out in the countryside. Hornsey Wood Tavern, with gardens and well-stocked fishing lake in its grounds, attracted people of all classes from the 18th century onwards, till in 1866 the house was demolished and the land absorbed into Finsbury Park, opened in 1869.

In Hornsey High Street The Three Compasses, a Georgian bow windowed building was a popular venue, with cricket played behind the pub and anglers fishing in the New River which wound round it. In 1852 this artificial water channel which since 1613 had brought fresh water to London from Hertfordshire springs was straightened, no longer to flow past the pub or to cross Hornsey High Street three times as it once did, and the character of the area began to change. Other Hornsey public houses visited by Londoners on holiday outings included The Nightingale in Nightingale Lane, an old world tavern with large gardens, quoits on the green in front, and country walks easily taken from it.

Publican of The Three Compasses, William Paulton, was a notable local character who wore a wide brimmed quaker hat. His name appears as landlord on a preserved poster advertising a cricket match in 1842 but he lived to 1888 and died aged 80. He is buried in the first grave by the footpath in Hornsey churchyard and the local saying was that this location was so that he could best knock for his pint — the pub not being far off, and indeed used by the parish vestry in earlier times for its meetings.

In the mid 19th century a nearby area was chosen as the location for a new recreational centre. North of the Priory estate, at the west end of Hornsey village, stretched the farmlands of Thomas Rhodes, most of them in the parish of Tottenham. After he died in 1856 plans by his heirs to develop the 400 acres for housing plots were supplanted by the purchase of the farm for the creation of a park and a People's Palace to rival the Crystal Palace in south London. Alexandra Park opened in 1863 and the Palace, built in the 1860s, was finally opened in 1873. Its chequered early history was marked by bankruptcies but its existence has meant that the parish of Hornsey has always been abutted on the north by open land rather than by housing estates, preserving to this day some 200 acres of open space. One of the recreations available in the park was horse racing on a course opened in 1868 which was to operate until September 1970. The Palace, burnt down soon after opening and then rebuilt, was to endure another fire in 1980. The half gutted building was carefully restored and improved and was opened again in 1988, though full rebuilding has not been completed due to lack of funds.

The Three Compasses in Hornsey High Street, a red brick Georgian inn photographed in 1873. Next to it is the newly built boys school and beyond it the ivy covered Hornsey Church tower. A public house of the same name replaced it in 1896.

Despite the racing, Hornsey as a place for a day out was to change with the expansion of London. The metropolis developed as a financial as well as a trading centre and in the days before typewriters, telephones and other aids to correspondence and accounting, it needed an army of clerks and administrators. In addition, London's many trades and industries helped make it the largest manufacturing city in the country. This growing population, stable economic conditions, a flexible building industry, the availability of capital and the reduction of hours of work which gave more travelling time were factors which aided the movement outwards of people into new places of residence. The trend was helped by a taste for privacy and a yearning for the countryside as a place in which to live.

The development of the suburbs was undertaken through many speculative ventures. Development of land depended in the first place upon the availability of estates. The erratic nature of suburban development is partly due to the reluctance of landowners to sell. But their desire to go on residing in places like Hornsey was undermined when neighbouring estates were sold, the character of the place altered and land rose in value. A verse published in Tarbuck's *Handbook of House Property* summarises the position:

'The richest crop for any field
Is a crop of bricks for it to yield,
The richest crop that it can grow
Is a crop of houses in a row.'

The developer often aimed to create the best quality suburban estate he could in expectation of higher rents and income. Economic pressures as the city moved outwards often thwarted this. Islington for example, was a village built up in the early 19th century for a middle class population but soon was largely taken over by an inner city working class. Larger houses were subdivided and density of occupation increased.

The key to the development of the suburbs lies in transport. It had been usual for a working man to walk to his job and Hornsey was too far out from London for this journey to be made there and back each day. Limited coach and omnibus services existed but even in the 1870s the bus fare from Hornsey to London Bridge was 6d (2½p) at a time when a skilled man's wages would be less than £1.50 per week. So it was only the middle classes who were able to live in Hornsey and travel to the city to work.

The invention of mechanical forms of transport, starting with the steam train and to encompass the tramway and the bicycle and later the petrol engine and electric traction, changed the position. The whole of London's hinterland, north and south of the Thames, and cities elsewhere were to be affected. Villages and towns in Middlesex, Essex and Surrey were to be absorbed in a blanket of houses, the fields obliterated by bricks and mortar. Survival of open space became a matter of chance, patronage or campaigning.

The 19th century began with the improvement of roads. Locally there had been Archway Road in 1813 and Seven Sisters turnpike road, developed in 1832 to improve access in and out of London. The turnpike system, with tolls paying for road maintenance was not affected by the 1835 General Highways Act and tolls were to continue into the later 19th century. The turnpike at the eastern end of Tottenham Lane led to the road being renamed Turnpike Lane, in due course (in 1932) giving its name to the underground tube station. Coach services out of

London were improved but they were limited by the capacity and speed of horses.

Railways were conceived for the long distance transport of freight, rivalling the canal system which started in the late 18th century. Passengers began to be taken on trains and then trains began to be used for shorter passenger journeys from outlying districts to the capital. This was profitable. More companies built lines and parliamentary acts authorising them started to make it obligatory for the operating companies to issue cheap workmen's fares to facilitate their use by lower paid workers, some of whom had been moved out of inner city homes to make way for the lines. The Cheap Trains Act of 1883 made this general and so facilitated clerks and other lower paid workers moving to new terraced homes in the suburbs built near the railway stations. The cheap fares were obtainable on the very early trains only.

The first of the railways to affect Hornsey parish was the Great Northern which in 1850 opened a service to the north, with Kings Cross as its terminus from 1852. This was the third of the major railway lines to be built to connect London with the principal provincial towns. The railway traversed the parish and the first station out of London was to be Hornsey. It was in a rural setting, on the east side of Hornsey village, with no bridge across the metals and the Railway Hotel nearby (since renamed) was a country inn with a spacious **tea garden.**

In 1861 in the south of the parish, by the boundary with Islington, a railway halt on the same GN line was opened and named Seven Sisters Road. In 1867 a branch line from there to East Finchley was opened with stations at Crouch End and Highgate. In 1869 when Hornsey Wood was renamed Finsbury Park the adjacent Seven Sisters Road halt was renamed Finsbury Park and greatly expanded as the railway system developed. Hornsey station was resited and rebuilt in 1866 and Harringay (West) opened between Hornsey and Finsbury Park in 1885 (now named Harringay). These changes followed the expansion from 1863 by the Great Northern of its railway services, creating a city and suburban service to Farringdon Street and increasing the number of trains from the previous seven or eight a day. In 1869 the service went beyond Farringdon Street to Moorgate and links with other railways led to a service to Victoria via Farringdon Street and Blackfriars.

In London itself, the main line termini at Paddington, Euston, Kings Cross, St. Pancras and Liverpool Street were connected from 1863 by the Metropolitan railway, the world's first underground system, operated by steam trains and at the end of the century to be electrified. This allowed suburban commuters to reach their places of work in the city and encouraged commerce to expand in the West End.

To the east of Hornsey the flat lands of Tottenham began to be covered by terraced housing largely occupied by clerks after the Liverpool Street to Enfield railway was planned. It opened in 1872 with stations at Seven Sisters, Bruce Grove and White Hart Lane. The Act granting it authority ruled that cheap fares should be provided. It was this railway rather than the 1840 Northern and Eastern line from Stratford to Broxbourne with stations at Tottenham Hale and Northumberland Park, or the Tottenham & Hampstead Junction line which opened in 1868, which led to the rapid transformation of Hornsey's neighbouring parish on the east. Stations on the Tottenham & Hampstead Junction line, which ran to Fenchurch Street, were to open at Crouch Hill in 1870 and in 1880 at Harringay Park, now Harringay (Green Lanes).

In 1873 a new branch line from Highgate to serve Alexandra Palace opened, with stations at the palace and at Muswell Hill, and in 1881 a station opened at Stroud Green on the line between Highgate and Finsbury Park.

Between the opening of Hornsey station in 1850 and that of Harringay West in 1885 some 10 railway stations became available in the area and it is in this period that real urbanisation began. One local man who would have watched it happen was Canon Richard Harvey (1801-1889), Rector of Hornsey, who held his appointment from 1829 to 1881 and thus lived to see his parish completely transformed. Canon Harvey was a notable local figure and Harvey Road is named after him. He was a tall man of aristocractic mien, said to have the eccentric habit of walking about with a handkerchief clutched in his teeth. But he was kind enough to carry laundry women's loaded baskets if he met them in the road. To celebrate his 50 years as Rector in 1879 he was presented with a large leather and brass bound book ornamented with the Harvey crest subscribed for by the parishioners, many of whom signed their names within. When he retired he became Canon Residentiary at Gloucester till his death in 1889. He and his wife died within 12 hours of each other, after 59 years of marriage.

In 1821, just before Canon Harvey came, there were only about 5,000 people in the parish, but the census shows that by 1861 there were 11,082 reflecting no doubt the influx of new villas and middle class residents in that period. But the age of 19th century villas and small estates in a rural setting was not to last very long. Terraced housing was to overwhelm them.

The population expanded persistently and enormously. In 1871 there were 19,357 people but by 1881 there were 37,078. Then in the next 10 years the numbers rose to 61,097. Even greater was the total by 1901 when there were 72,056 inhabitants. By 1911 there were 84,592 and by 1921 Hornsey had 87,659 people in what had become from 1903 a Middlesex borough. In effect what was created in the parish in the last quarter of the 19th century was a large new town

Looking Down, Muswell Hill.

Muswell Hill railway station sited down hill next to The Green Man and opened in 1873 on the new line to Alexandra Palace. Since 1966 its site has been occupied by a school and the line converted into the Parkland Walk. By courtesty of Dick Whetstone.

as big as many provincial cities. In the 20 years between 1881 and 1901 some 60,000 new inhabitants arrived in Hornsey, some by birth, but most by immigration. At the same time the green fields were covered with terraced houses.

The growth was part of the spread north of London's built environment. To the south of Hornsey its neighbour Islington experienced its heaviest decades of building from 1841 to 1861. With increasing density of occupation Islington's population increased from 95,329 in 1851 to 282,865 in 1881. Also to the south Stoke Newington's population in 1871 of just under 10,000 rose to 22,781 in 1881 and 30,936 in 1901. To the east Tottenham increased from 13,240 in 1861 to 46,456 in 1881 and 97,124 in 1891.

In such a situation the preservation of open spaces is an important matter. Campaigns led to the preservation in Hornsey of Highgate Woods in 1886 and of Queens Woods in 1894 and both Alexandra Park and Coldfall Woods were

View from Shepherds Hill looking north across Crouch End playing fields to Alexandra Palace and Park. These large open spaces have continued to be preserved. By courtesy of Dick Whetstone.

saved from development. Finsbury Park, opened in 1869, gave 120 acres of space in the south east and Clissold Park in South Hornsey was opened in 1886. Crouch End playing fields were acquired in 1892 and by 1926 had been enlarged to 40 acres. This is more open space than is to be found in London suburban areas to the south, and, with its trees and elevation, probably helped Hornsey establish its reputation for being healthy, with the lowest death rate in the country in 1905.

The open spaces help keep alive the memory of Hornsey parish as a green place. Even in 1875 this rural image persisted, as James Thorne in his *Handbook to the Environs of London* shows. He describes Hornsey village as:

'... long, irregular and scattered. By the church, the character is preserved in the lanes that run off from it, as it is in the extension of the main street towards Muswell Hill. Along the lanes villas rise on every side. The New River meanders in devious fashion through the valley. The fields, although fast diminishing, are still pleasant, and the heights on either hand afford wide prospects. The new Alexandra Palace is of course conspicuous from all of them.'

Thorne writes that: 'Crouch End ... has still some pretty rural lanes, like that to Stroud Green and good old brick houses, but all available sites are being fast built over. Christ Church, on high ground at the S. end of the hamlet, near Hornsey Lane, was erected in 1863 ... a tower with stone spire added in 1873.'

Thorne's reference to available sites being fast built over must have been unhappy daily knowledge to local people. In 1881 the *Hornsey and Finsbury Park Journal* is commenting:

'It is clear that the doom of Hornsey is settled. Not much longer will it remain the quiet and secluded village of which everyone has heard ... protestations come too late now. Hornsey is to be given up to the builders ... No more will the village baker walk his regular round ... he will drive his four wheeled vehicle to cut up the roads, splash mud on pedestrians and expedite his business. Coal merchants will cling to the outskirts of railway stations and milliners will advertise the latest Regent Street fashions'.

The countryside was to become a town.

How Hornsey was built up

Urbanisation was to affect the existing settlements of Hornsey village, Crouch End, Highgate and finally Muswell Hill, enlarging them and eventually joining them together. It also changed the comparatively empty south of the parish. Building developments there began in the 1860s when a new estate was created south of Seven Sisters Road called Brownswood Park on 156 acres of previously undeveloped land. By 1894 there were 1,077 houses on the estate.

North of Seven Sisters Road the only houses on the north east (Hornsey) side of hedged Stroud Green Lane were Stapleton House and the little recorded Japan House (where Japan Crescent now is). When in 1867 the branch line was added to the Seven Sisters Road halt the area near the expanding station began to be built up. Stroud Green Farm and Hornsey Wood Farm disappear from the map and the open country which existed in 1861 north of Seven Sisters Road is covered with streets. Similar development occurred on the Islington side of

Stroud Green Road, south of Hanley Road. Frank How, whose memories of the area are in *HHS Bulletin no. 25* records that it was still rural in 1875, with a maypole set up in Ennis Road, attended by Jack-in-the-Green. But by this time Finsbury Park was recognised as a distinct suburb with its own newspaper.

Hornsey village also saw building developments begin in the 1860s. By the 1870s some 1,300 houses had been built in new estates which pushed urban fingers north and south of the old village. This had been possible following the acquisition of Grove House and its neighbour on the corner of Middle Lane and High Street, and of Campsbourne Lodge on the north side.

The loss of Campsbourne Lodge was typical of the disappearance of 'good old houses'. Campsbourne had comprised about seven acres of ornamental gardens, a lake of one acre and about 12 acres of meadows. Probably occupied since medieval times, the first recorded owner had been city merchant Sir John Skevington, who died in 1525. The last owner was a diamond merchant, William Eady. Two years after his death in 1865 the estate was sold to the British Land Company who pulled down the Lodge and built streets of small houses over the once strikingly beautiful grounds. The name fortunately survives.

East of Hornsey village the Hornsey Park estate was built close to new gasworks put up in Clarendon Road in 1865. Streets began to be lit by gas supplied by the Hornsey gas company from 1869, but lamps were sparse in number. By 1863 filter beds and a water pumping station had been built on the west side of the GNR line. A decade earlier the New River Company (which in 1904 was to be absorbed into the Metropolitan Water Board) had built filter beds and a pumping station beside the New River in South Hornsey later incorporated into Stoke Newington.

Building near the church, such as the St. Mary's estate, began in the 1870s but the rector resisted development of the glebe land to the south of the church, and by 1896 it was only partly built up. Part of this land was used in 1848 when a National infants school was established in Tottenham Lane. This building, with a subsequent enlargement demolished, and somewhat altered, is now the headquarters of the Hornsey Historical Society. Adjacent to this site, a new church to serve the expanding district was built in 1877 and named Holy Innocents.

Across Tottenham Lane, in the valley which exists between the GNR and Ferme Park Road, an enclave of houses, collectively known as Hornsey Vale was built. This is described in *HHS Bulletin no. 29*. Over 200 terraced houses were built there by 1880. To the north the builder J. C. Hill developed Rathcoole estate and house which fronted Tottenham Lane, and other land there, with 257

Hornsey Wood House was a genteel tea house on the edge of Hornsey Wood but in 1796 was extended to become Hornsey Wood House Tavern with enlarged gardens and a lake for fishing. Demolished in 1866, the grounds were absorbed into Finsbury Park.

terraced houses planned for Rathcoole Avenue, Rathcoole Gardens and Harvey and Uplands Roads, though few had been built before 1896. Ferme Park Road was constructed over the Hogs Back ridge from Stroud Green in 1880. Previously this area had been farmland and the ridge itself occupied by a number of houses such as Womersley House, home of Peter Robinson, the Oxford Street draper. The district west of Ferme Park road was built over by 1896.

In Hornsey High Street further building continued in the 1870s, 1880s and 1890s. Resulting from the Enclosure Award, a common still existed in the mid 19th century in the village, stretching from the churchyard to The Three Compasses. It was divided from the road by railings and used by locals to dry washing. The green still exists. In 1872, facing it, St. Mary's School for Boys was built. It replaced an earlier school in Priory Road and was designed to obviate the need for a Board School under the 1870 Education Act. Its site is now the playground of present day St. David's and St. Katherine's school, built in the late 1970s.

Opposite the green a new Victorian gin palace, The Great Northern Railway Tavern, now an admired piece of architecture, was put up in 1897 to replace an old tavern near long surviving Eagle Cottage. In one of four wooden houses between this house and the water company's land lived Mr. Crouch, the last Beadle of the old parish church, a terror to the children of the nieghbourhood. His flowing robe, later reduced to a coat, was blue with gold lace and he wore a yellow wig and a three cornered hat.

On the south side, The Three Compasses was rebuilt in 1896, and a three-storeyed terrace of shops, The Pavement, put up. It was in 1870, in 32 High Street, that Mrs. Ann Greig had started selling cooked meat. Her son David Greig was to make his name nationally known for his provision shops. In October 1929 he was to be made the first honorary freeman of Hornsey borough. By his bequest the Greig charitable trust continues to help the needy and to endow various community enterprises in the area.

Harringay, built on the east side of Hornsey village, alongside Green Lanes, takes its name from the vanished estate of Harringay House mentioned earlier. (The way of spelling it differently from Haringey, chosen as the name of the new London Borough some seventy years later, causes confusion to some). Thorne recorded Harringay House in 1875 as being the seat of W.C. Alexander, Esq., but within a decade the large estate was acquired by the British Land Company. It was laid out on a grid plan with 23 roads, with Wightman Road forming the west side. It was to have two churches and two schools (in 1893 in Frobisher Road and in 1904 in Mattison Road) as well as swimming baths. By 1899 the estate comprised 2,400 houses, many of them inhabited by clerks. The old mansion did not sell when marketed and was demolished as the estate was built. So disappeared one of the last of the big houses with substantial grounds in Hornsey. The estate is popularly known as the Harringay ladder.

Crouch End was to have New Road laid out with properties in the angle between Middle Lane and Park Road in 1854 and Haringey Park, off Crouch Hill, in 1861 where 15 large houses were built, 25 in 1871. Christ Church was built in 1863. But it was not until the 1880s that Crouch End assumed its modern appearance as one large house after another went.

Crouch Hall, on the west side of what is now the Broadway, was one of the largest estates. It comprised nearly 10 acres. Its lake, parallel to the road, covered two acres. The house was occupied up to 1845 by John Gillyat Booth of the gin family and the lake was known to locals as Lake Geneva (gin was sometimes called geneva by the ill informed, but it had no connection with that city, the name of gin deriving from *ginevra,* the Italian word for juniper which was added for flavouring). The last owner of Crouch Hall was William Bird JP, steelmaster

Crouch End Broadway with Topsfield Hall, demolished in 1894, still to be seen in the distance. The newly erected late 19th century buildings denote the urbanisation of the village centre.

and member of the Local Board. When the Imperial Property Company bought the estate in 1882 the local wits said that the Birds had flown. The hall was demolished in 1884, and Crouch Hall Road built across the grounds. Shops were built on the Broadway, amongst them J.H. Wilson's drapery store, established in 1896, which lasted into the 1960s. Also bought by the property company and demolished was the adjacent Crouch End Academy on the corner of Park Road, the three storeyed weather boarded house, possibly dated from the 17th century when schooling first began there.

Also to disappear from Crouch End in the 1880s were Lindslade House and Old Crouch Hall, both in 1888. The latter was replaced by Bank Buildings on the corner of Weston Park. Weston Park, Bourne Road, Landrock Road and Gladwell Road had been laid out by 1884.

Local street names derive from City brush merchant Henry Weston Elder (d. 1882) who occupied the old manor house, Topsfield Hall, at the junction of Middle and Tottenham Lanes. The final turning point for Crouch End came with the sale of the land owned by his widow, Mrs. Sarah Elder. The property included the smithy, pub, chapel and cottages at the foot of Crouch Hill. The smithy was replaced by a bank (later rebuilt) and other new buildings. (The pub was rebuilt in its present form in 1892). Topsfield Hall was demolished in 1895 and replaced by Topsfield Parade, erected by James Edmondson of Highbury.

A similar parade of shops was built on the other side of Tottenham Lane by the builder J.C. Hill who also laid out Felix Avenue and Fairfield Gardens and in 1898 erected the Queens Hotel, a surviving and admired piece of Art Nouveau architecture. Houses were for sale in Cecile Park and Elder Avenue by 1892 to designs by J. Farrer, the architect responsible for much new housing in the district, after whom Farrer Road, off Priory Road is named.

The opening of the station on Crouch Hill in 1867 had led to further building in Hornsey Lane and the construction of Crescent Road round the church, which in 1873 was improved by the addition of its plain broach spire. In the same year Mr. Bird laid out Edison Road on his land off Crouch Hill and gave a site for a Sunday school. Gradually Crouch End began to fill with houses. Between 1882 and 1892 some 400 were built, many in Gothic revival styles.

Land had been acquired for development between Crouch End and Highgate in the 1870s and in the 1880s Stanhope Road, between Crescent Road and Shephers Hill was built up. Crouch End and Highgate were both considered 'good' residential areas and houses in the Coolhurst Road area, where 12 roads had been laid out by 1882, were of high quality. This was acquired by the Imperial Property Investment Company who extended to Park Road and called their land Imperial Park (it is so marked on the 1894 Ordnanace Survey map) but development of this estate was slow and the name disappeared.

Highgate continued to develop, both the parts inside and outside Hornsey parish. Following the 1867 opening of the Highgate railway station at the junction of Archway Road and the northern extension of Southwood Lane, which by the 1880s was named Muswell Hill Road, new housing was put up, filling the area between the railway and Archway Road. By the 1890s the Miltons area in the southern part were built. Shepherds Hill became a road instead of a bridle path and began to have large houses on its south side by 1882.

On the west side of Archway Road stood Winchester Hall, on the corner of Hornsey Lane and Highgate Hill. A house had stood on this site at least from the 17th century, its name possibly a pun on that of Susanna Winch, a widow once resident there. From the 1860s the house was occupied by John William Jeakes and his family; he ran a successful furnishing ironmongery business and became a JP and chairman of Hornsey Local Board. He died suddenly at the age of 57 in 1874 and by 1881 his family had sold the Hall to the Imperial Property Investment Company. Winchester Road and Cromwell Avenue, terraced streets, were built on the grounds as well as Winchester Place. A large new public house built in Archway Road at the same time was named Winchester Hall Tavern.

Increased traffic on the Archway Road meant that the narrow archway which carried Hornsey Lane across was an impediment and it was rebuilt under powers obtained in 1894 by the London County Council. The single span bridge, designed by the LCC's chief engineer, Sir Alexander Binnie, was built next to the old arch which was then dismantled. The new bridge was opened in 1900.

At the end of the century the Warner lands in Priory Road were developed according to plans drawn up by J. Farrer. The Priory was demolished in 1902, and roads laid out towards Alexandra Park for terraced houses, as well as on the south side of Priory Road. Housing along Park Road towards Priory Road developed and from 1902 farmland between the two roads began to be built over, so that Crouch End and Hornsey began to meet. But building south of Hornsey village towards Crouch End along Middle Lane was impeded by the grounds of the comparatively new Rokesly House, Hermiston Lodge and Elm House.

Local government provision

It is impossible to detail each Victorian road which transformed the rural setting of Hornsey, Crouch End, Stroud Green, Highgate and Muswell Hill into an urban one in those dramatic decades. A lot of research remains to be undertaken into the work of many building firms, and also into the origins and occupations of the people who came to live in the new houses. What should be borne in mind, however, is that to lay out new roads and to build houses are only the first steps in the creation of a new community.

Builders are bound by regulations which over the centuries have come to control their work in the interests of the local people generally as well as the occupants of what they build. The important 1875 Public Health Act laid down conditions, such as the width new residential roads should be, the amount of light and space provided in a house, and the necessary sanitary facilities in an age when flush toilets and sewers were replacing cesspools and when piped water was being supplied for the first time on a regular basis.

Building a suburb is more even than arranging a water supply, sewage disposal, lighting and power supplies. Services are needed, including shops, schools, transport, recreational amenities and churches. Roads must be regularly cleaned, people and property protected by a fire service and a police force, public health safeguarded and diseases contained, with hospitals and doctors available for the sick. The 19th century witnessed the growth of voluntary services and local government provision to deal with these matters for a rapidly growing population.

Hornsey's local government had to change as the district changed. In 1865 a local board of health was established for South Hornsey, the 230 acre district south of Seven Sisters Road, under the 1858 Local Government Act. Only in 1867 was Hornsey Local Board established, catering for the remaining 2,809 acres of the parish. The two boards were autonomous. South Hornsey was eventually, in 1900, to be incorporated in the new Borough of Stoke Newington, so that from the 1860s its story is different from Hornsey proper.

These new local boards were an attempt to deal with urban problems, especially sanitation and health, which the vestry was too amateur a body to tackle properly. A local newspaper at this time commented that Hornsey was the worst governed parish in London. It had resisted the creation of a local board of health as it had resisted other changes such as railway development, realignment of the New River, inclusion in the metropolitan police district and in the metropolitan sewage system. It also objected to the proposed boundary rationalisation in the south of the parish.

The new Local Board used the offices in Highgate High Street which accommodated the highways board, but in 1869 moved into purpose-built premises at 99 Southwood Lane. These offices, which were to be enlarged, continued to be used for local government administration until 1934 when Hornsey Town Hall was built in Crouch End.

Local boards of health gave way to new forms of local councils. Under the Local Government Act 1894 Hornsey acquired an Urban District Council and in 1903 became a Borough in the county of Middlesex. The various initials HLB, HUDC and BH which are to be found on hydrant gratings and street furniture can be used as clues to the development of particular areas.

The proceedings of the council can be traced in the official minutes or in contemporary local newspaper reports which highlight the problems they dealt with. The urban district council had power to control estate development and builders needed to submit road and house plans to the authority for approval. These records can help inquirers discover when particular road and estates were conceived. For example, at the Council meeting on 6th March 1899, plans were approved as follows:

'For laying out the frontage of the Priory Estate to the north of Priory Road and for private carriage drives running parallel to Priory Road, Hornsey by Mr. John Farrer, surveyor of Finsbury Pavement E.C. ... For three dwelling houses in Kings Avenue, Muswell Hill by Mr. Woolnough of Branstone Road, Crouch End ... for one dwelling house in Hillfield Park, Muswell Hill, by Messrs. Edmondson of Station Parade, Muswell Hill ... for laying out part of the Priory Estate on the south side of Priory Road, Hornsey by Mr. Farrer, conditional on his furnishing evidence to the Council's satisfaction that the owner of the adjoining land on the south side had agreed to the proposed give and take new boundary and the giving up of a portion of land at the junction of Park and Priory Road for the purpose of widening the highway'.

Chairman of Hornsey Local Board for 10 years and founder of the local Liberal party, was wine merchant Herbert Reader Williams (1822-97). He launched a campaign through *The Times* to save Highgate Woods. He also pursued other causes. The clock tower in Crouch End Broadway was put up in his honour in his lifetime. The portrait and description on it can still be seen despite traffic hazards and the addition of underground public toilets. The obituary for H.R. Williams in the *Hornsey Journal* of 2nd October, 1897 records that it was almost entirely due to his exertions that the southern side of Alexandra Park was saved from the clutches of the speculative builder. His concern would have been encouraged by his being the occupant of the Priory (in fact the last) whose estates abutted the south side of the park.

Another local councillor was Henry Burt, the driving force behind the UDC libraries, with Hornsey Central Library in Tottenham Lane opening next to Hornsey police station 1899, Stroud Green opening in 1901 and Highgate in 1902. Councillor Burt was also largely responsible for the purchase in 1901 of Alexandra Park and Palace by a consortium of local authorities.

The urban district council had eight wards, each of which elected three councillors. It not only had control over planning and road layout (a minimum 40ft width was required) but also over sewerage and drainage, public baths, wash-houses, parks and open spaces, and could appoint a local medical officer of health and a surveyor. One activity it pursued was the planting of trees to help restore Hornsey's once verdant appearance. By 1896 it had planted 2,859 trees. In its review of 1896-1900 the UDC recorded that it had planted 3,383 additional trees, of which 1,437 were planes. In those three and a half years it approved seven miles of new roads and put 40 carts and vans into operation to water streets. Its policy was not to make up streets until two thirds of the length of the road had been built upon.

Council housing began with permissive legislation at the end of the 19th century. Hornsey UDC seems to have been one of the first local councils to take advantage of the new legislation, deciding in January 1896 to adopt the 1890 Housing of the Working Classes Act and to purchase $4\frac{1}{2}$ acres of land at Hornsey to erect self-contained cottages. By 1899 roads and buildings close to the Board school at the top of Nightingale Lane, adjacent to Alexandra Park, had been established at a total cost of £31,000. Within a few years more roads were added to this estate. In Nightingale Lane the old pub was rebuilt and some old cottages demolished.

The council houses were for rent, for this was the predominant way houses were occupied until well into the 20th century, even amongst the middle classes. The availability of rented accommodation aided the mobility of labour as people moved into the new urban areas from the surrounding countryside or from the inner cities. It was only after the first World War that the movement towards owner-occupier tenure began to quicken, aided by building society growth.

Although it was situated in Middlesex, Hornsey was affected by the creation of the new county of London in 1888. The London County Council's domain reached as far as the southern boundary of Hornsey at Hornsey Lane and continued over the Archway crossroads up Highgate Hill and into Kenwood. In the 20th century the LCC was to purchase land on the fringes of London in order to establish housing estates. LCC estates were built in Islington, south of Hornsey Lane and in neighbouring Tottenham at White Hart Lane.

Increased population led to greater parliamentary representation for Middlesex, which had returned two Commons members since the Middle Ages. Under the 1885 Redistribution of Seats Acts Middlesex was split into seven divisions with one constituency consisting of the parishes of Finchley and Hornsey, including South Hornsey, plus the freeholders, of the City of London, Finsbury and Islington who in 1907 numbered 7,000 outvoters. In 1918 the Representation of People Act abolished the outvoter rights and made the municipal borough into a parliamentary borough.

The Edwardian era

In the 1890s Muswell Hill was the last surviving village in Hornsey parish. The coming of a railway station on the Hill in the 1870s when the Palace opened had led to the Grove and neighbouring Bath House being demolished and three-storey Victorian terraced housing being built there, and to Alexandra Gardens and Muswell Hill Place opposite the station being laid out with building plots. But development was slow, despite the railway. Service was often suspended whilst the Palace was closed, and the rural nature of Muswell Hill was preserved.

The land east of Colney Hatch Lane owned by the nuns had passed into lay ownership at the dissolution of religious houses by Henry VIII and had come under the civil jurisdiction of the vestry of St. James's church, Clerkenwell where the nunnery had been situated. The area became known as Clerkenwell Detached. Roads began to be laid out on it in the 1880s but the take-up of plots was slow and only 54 houses had been built by 1891.

Separation from Hornsey had led to problems of sewage disposal and to disputes over road paving. Clerkenwell resisted approaches from Hornsey UDC to take over control and marked out the boundaries of the 64 detached acres with distinctive iron boundary markers (one is preserved in the Tetherdown institute's hall, and another at Bruce Castle). But following the London Government Act 1899 enabling local boundaries to be adjusted, and an enquiry, Clerkenwell Detached was returned to Hornsey in 1900. At the enquiry it was said that 50 acres had been laid out ready for building, that there were 209 houses erected, 161 being occupied and the estimated population was 1,086 persons. An 1898 proposal by Clerkenwell to preserve the old well as an historic relic never came to fruition.

The division of local authority control might have been one reason for the late development of Muswell Hill, as well as the hilly terrain and the reluctance of local owners to sell. Its development is sometimes attributed to an 1896 murder which brought thousands of people to Muswell Hill to see Muswell Lodge, the villa where an elderly man had been killed during the course of a midnight robbery. But a more practical reason for its sudden change was that The Limes, once the home of C.E. Mudie (1818-90), pioneer of private circulating libraries, came up for sale.

The purchaser was James Edmondson & Sons of Highbury, who had just erected Topsfield Parade in Crouch End. Within a very short time most of the other villas and estates in the centre of Muswell Hill were sold as residents moved out in the face of change. The subsequent development of Muswell Hill as a select suburb with its characteristic building style of large terraced houses with stone dressings and pargeting work is due to James Edmondson. Queens Avenue

Athenaeum, Muswell Hill built in 1900 by James Edmondson in Fortis Green Road to provide concert halls for the new suburb. It was used for many social activities. In the 1960s it was replaced by a branch of J. Sainsbury. By courtesy of Dick Whetstone.

was laid out by him across the Limes estate and Queens Parade of shops was built in 1897 along the line of Muswell Hill Road as the start of the well-known Muswell Hill Broadway shopping centre. In July 1897 the *Hornsey Journal* recorded that the footway along the front of the new shops was being asphalted and in August 1897 that some of the shops were opened. Martyn's grocery (now no. 135) has continued in operation there ever since, still with its original mahogany shop fittings.

With the neighbouring Fortis House estate James Edmondson had acquired 30 acres on the hilltop plateau. He laid out Princes Avenue across this estate, and on its boundary in Fortis Green Road he built St. James's Parade of shops in 1900 and Princes Parade. Edmondson extended his holdings by acquiring North Lodge and Wellfield estates in Colney Hatch Lane where more shopping parades and a postal sorting office were built, The Elms at the top of of Muswell Hill by the present day roundabout, where he created the semi-circular shopping parades known as the Exchange — and developed Dukes Avenue on what was first known as the Station estate.

Edmondson gave the sites on which the Congregational church in Queens Avenue and the Baptist church in Dukes Avenue were to be built, and offered a site for a library, as well as providing assembly rooms in Fortis Green Road in an imposing building known as the Athenaeum. In contrast, no public houses were built and local residents had to make do with the Green Man which had stood at the top of Muswell Hill from at least Tudor times, the diminutive, weather-boarded Royal Oak in St. James's Lane, or the public houses in Fortis Green. Here in 1900 Fortis Green Brewery was to disappear (but not its pub, The Clissold) and was replaced by a 1904 police station.

The other chief developer in the suburb was William Jefferies Collins (1856-1939), a speculative builder who bought land for development and used his own labour force of about 30 men to build very good quality houses. Across his properties, Fortismere and The Firs, between Fortis Green Road and Fortis Green, he laid out Grand Avenue and five other terraced avenues. He built Church Crescent and other roads and then began to develop the Rookfield estate which he had purchased in 1899 and moved into as a place of residence.

This estate on the south side of Muswell Hill, near the junction with Park Road, also accommodated Avenue House and Lalla Rookh. Collins began to build traditional houses on the side of the hill and in Etheldene Avenue, a new road laid out on the south side of the estate. In 1911 he moved away to the Southampton area where he continued his building enterprises and the development of the estate was left to two of his sons, Herbert (1885-1975) and William Brannan Collins (1883-1977), known as 'Billy'. Rookfield Garden Estate was built by the sons under the influence of garden city ideas, with irregular groupings of houses, communal open space, lower densities and vernacular house styles in new architectural modes. Anne Trevett writes about this estate in *HHS Bulletin no. 29*.

Muswell Hill also developed on the south side towards Highgate. Cranley Gardens railway station, to serve this area, was opened on the branch line to the Palace in 1902. Fortis Green retained its 19th century village appearance, with the Harwell Estate, comprising Eastern, Western and Southern Roads slowly built up and St. James's school of 1850 extended to meet increasing numbers of children. Near the school in Fortis Green was built a fire station and land behind was acquired for a council depot. St. James's church itself, established on its site in 1842 and later extended, proved to be too small and too much in need of repair, and it was replaced in the Edwardian period by the present church. By

1914 there existed a new suburb, served by churches and public services, inhabited for the most part by people who travelled by train or bus to London to work, some of whom on their return used the numerous tennis courts and bowling clubs or attended social events in the Athenaeum, such as meetings of the 'Muswell Hill Parliament'.

Hornsey since 1914

By the time of the first World War, Hornsey had been mostly built up. Little land was left for development, though some occurred, such as the reduction in size of Coldfall Woods, purchased by the borough and used for council housing, as well as for private housing development north of Fortis Green. Additional brick built blocks of flats were put up by the Collins family including the set at the junction of Fortis Green Road and Fortis Green. A 1920s block of flats replaced Woodside house opposite on the corner with Tetherdown, but most of the large old houses had gone in the borough.

In Hornsey village in 1920 old wooden shops and Preston's and Allen's courts gave way for the council's bath and wash-houses, to give the High Street something more of its modern appearance. In Crouch End, Oakfield Villa was replaced by a new telephone exchange and Oakfield House by Oakfield Court in 1937. In Tottenham Lane the terraced shops and cottages of Manor Place were pulled down in 1935. In 1934 Hornsey village was at last linked with Crouch End along Middle Lane when Elmfield Avenue and part of Hermiston Avenue as well as Rokesly school were built over the Elm House and Rokesly House grounds to join with Rokesly Avenue which had been built on the same estate from 1909.

Cinemas appeared, and notable amongst these was the Muswell Hill Odeon, still surviving and now listed for its Grade II Art Deco interior. Ironically this was built in 1936, the year that the world's first high definition regular public television service began to be operated in part of Alexandra Palace, the medium which was to replace cinema as mass entertainment. Cinemas which existed in the borough which have since disappeared included the 1911 Picture House in Tottenham Lane Crouch End, succeeded in 1922 by the Perfect renamed in 1930 as the Plaza; the Rink on the corner of Stroud Green and Seven Sisters Roads renamed in 1950 the Gaumont; the Summerland in Muswell Hill Broadway which operated from 1921 to 1938; and the Ritz at the top of Muswell Hill later renamed the ABC. There were also cinemas in the Hippodrome in Topsfield Parade, in the National Hall in Hornsey High Street and in the Athenaeum, Muswell Hill at different periods of time.

The greatest change in the appearance of Hornsey has probably resulted from the impact of motorised road vehicles. The suburb was built in the days of horse-drawn road vehicles and since stables had not been provided with the houses space for garages has not been available for the new form of transport. With the arrival of private and commercial motorised transport the visual appearance of the streets has been altered by the advent of parked cars and continuous traffic moving at speed.

One benefit from motorised transport has been improved road surfacing. Early self-propelled vehicles were resented because people and property were smothered in dry weather by the huge clouds of road dust which they stirred up. From 1910 onwards roads thoughout the country slowly began to be given a new road crust in the shape of tarmac, an Edwardian invention which mixed tar and slag. The cost of the work was aided by a Road Fund administered by a Road Board set up by Lloyd George, the money coming from the tax on petrol and the annual road licence which, as Chancellor of the Exchequer, he had introduced in his 1909 budget. Tarmac also rid the country of muddy winter roads, and with the gradual disappearance of the horse (although horse-drawn milk, coal and railway carts were still to be seen in the 1960s) made the roads much cleaner. Doorstep boot wipers and paved road crossings for pedestrians at junctions —some of which can still be seen — were made obsolete.

In the 1920s and 1930s car ownership was restricted to the better-off because of the cost. But coach and bus services rapidly developed making the period a golden age for public transport. Commercial road transport also expanded with pneumatic tyres and enclosed drivers' cabins on vans coming into general use in the late 1920s and lightweight chassis aiding long distance delivery services. By 1934 Hore-Belisha had introduced road safety measures to help cut down the rising tide of casualties and the borough began to have pedestrian crossings with Belisha beacons, improved road signs and stricter speed limits.

Among the transport changes were electric-driven trams which appeared on Hornsey's roads from Edwardian times. A service for example ran from Turnpike Lane to Priory Road, with single deck cars going up into Alexandra Park. The metal tramway tracks were sunk into the granite sets of the roads and power was supplied from overhead electric cables, whose posts, along with those for telephone cables, also changed the suburb's appearance. Seven Sisters Road was busy with services and the area round Finsbury Park was a hub with a swirl of activity as crowds of people leaving the station sought to catch a tram or bus home.

Finsbury Park station had become from 1904 the terminus of an underground train service to Moorgate (Northern Line) and from 1906 for a similar service to connected Archway station (then called Highgate) with Charing Cross from 1907. Finsbury Park services were to expand between the wars with the extension in 1932 of the Piccadilly Line along the eastern side of Hornsey via Manor House, Turnpike Lane, Wood Green and Bounds Green out to Cockfosters, with well designed stations by Charles Holden. The improved travel facility led to the creation of new inter-war suburbs and also helped fill up pockets of land in Hornsey and Wood Green.

Hornsey in the 1920s and 1930s could be categorised as a mainly middle-class borough where servants, deliveries by tradesmen and respectable living were the order of the day. But as Joan Schwitzer's account of manual workers in Hornsey in *HHS Bulletin no. 27* reminds us, the area also relied on its working population to maintain its existence as a community. With housing in the Campsbourne, Northview, Coldfall, Hornsey Vale and other areas, a sizeable working population were engaged in service work, such as shops, laundries and in a number of small manufacturing establishments. These included piano and organ factories, sweets and chocolate manufacture, light engineering and small workshops. Long hours, hard work and low wages were common. But Hornsey was a diverse community which engendered strong local loyalties.

One notable flagship for the borough was its new town hall, built in 1934 in Crouch End Broadway. The site had been occupied in the 19th century by Lake Villa and Broadway Hall, the latter destroyed by fire in 1923. The borough acquired this smallish piece of land in 1920 and in 1923 laid it out as a park. The town hall was the subject of an architectural competition and posed difficult site problems. The winner was New Zealander R.H. Uren (1906-88) who designed a distinctive building said to be influenced by the Dutch architect W.H. Dudok. Described as a landmark for Britain in its recognition of the modern architectural movement of the time, it was to win a Royal Institute of British Architects award. During 1935-37 the site to the south was used to build gas showrooms and on the north the former telephone exchange was converted into electricity showrooms, so that by 1939 an harmonious civic complex existed.

This essay ends with Hornsey in 1939. Its story over the next decades remains to be told. During that time its fabric has suffered war damage and new buildings have replaced older ones. In 1939 the people who lived in Hornsey, with few exceptions, had not lived there for many generations; for the most part Hornsey in the period then was occupied by the children and grandchildren of immigrants from other counties and other parts of London. They were denizens of a new town, created in the countryside, a rural parish that had become a London suburb. Hornsey's population since then has not stood still. Some of the terraced streets have been redeveloped with blocks of flats and many people have come to settle here from overseas. For some residents Hornsey is just a dormitory from where they go to work in London. But for many others Hornsey is home, a place which they know and love and want to conserve.

46

Acknowledgements and further reading

Much of the information in this essay is from the *Victoria County History of Middlesex* (OUP for University of London). Volume VI (1980) includes Hornsey. Volume V (1976) covers Tottenham. I have also drawn upon information printed in the *Hornsey Historical Society Bulletin* which contains many illustrated articles based on detailed research. Highgate has been well covered in books and has been given less detailed attention in this essay to avoid it dominating the story of Hornsey. John Richardson's 286-page, most attractive *Highgate – Its History since the 15th century* (1983 Historical Publications, Barnet) has a full bibliography.

The text refers to the work of Dr. S.J. Madge. The volumes which he wrote were: *The Origins of the Name of Hornsey* (1936), *The Early Records of Harringay alias Hornsey* (1938) and *The Mediaeval Records of Harringay alias Hornsey 1216-1307* (1939). All three were published for the Public Libraries Committee of the Borough of Hornsey. In association with the Hornsey Historical Society the London Borough of Haringey published *Lost Houses of Harringey* (1986). Among the residences covered are Harringay House, Topsfield Hall, Campsbourne, The Grove (Muswell Hill) and Winchester Hall.

Hornsey Historical Society publications include a series of *Walks* covering Hornsey Village, Crouch End, Muswell Hill, Highgate and Kenwood Boundaries indicating surviving buildings of note. Other titles are: *How Haringey Grew* by Ian Murray (1985), *Rails to the People's Palace* by Reg Davies (1994 revised edition). *Palace on the Hill* by Ken Gay (1994 revised edition) and *The Little School* by Joan Schwitzer (1994). Books of old photographs, postcard views and reprints of early Ordnance Survey maps are also published by the society.

Middlesex by Michael Robbins (1953 Collins) is a good history of the county and its economic development and has an extensive bibliography. *A History of London* by Robert Gray (1978 Hutchinson — paperback) is a good general introduction. Also recommended are *London – the infernal Wen 1808-1870* by Francis Sheppard (1971 Secker), and the four volume series on *The Making of Modern London* (1983-86 Sidgwick & Jackson) published following a television series on London's development from 1815 to 1985. *Semi-Detached London* by Alan A. Jackson (1973 George Allen & Unwin) and *A History of London Transport* by T.C. Barker and Michael Robbins (2 vols 1963 and 1974 George Allen & Unwin) provide useful source material. *The English Terraced House* by Stefan Muthesius (1982 Yale) brings out the changing nature of house design. *Kings Bishop* by Barbara Denny (1985 The Alderman Press) tells the story of the Bishops of London.